By Christy Steele

Steadwell Books

Raintree Steck-Vaughn Publishers
A Harcourt Company

Austin · New York
www.steck-vaughn.com

ANIMALS OF THE RAIN FOREST

Published by Raintree Steck-Vaughn Publishers, an imprint of Steck-Vaughn Company.

Library of Congress Cataloging-in-Publication Data
   Sloths/by Christy Steele.
      p.cm.—(Animals of the rain forest)
      Includes bibliographical references (p.31).
      ISBN 0-7398-4683-3
      1. Sloths—Juvenile literature. [1. Sloths.] I. Title. II. Animals of the rain forest.
QL737.E2 S74 2001
599.3'13—dc21

                                                    2001019820

Printed and bound in the United States of America
1 2 3 4 5 6 7 8 9 10 WZ 05 04 03 02 01

Produced by Compass Books

Photo Acknowledgments
Corbis/Michael & Patricia Fogden, 12, 22; Kevin Schafer, 16. Visuals Unlimited, 24; Jim Merli, cover; A. Kerstitch, title page; Larry Kimball, 6; Kiell B. Sandved, 8; Jane McAlonan, 11; Barbara Magnuson, 14; Inga Spence, 18; Richard Thom, 20; Bruce Clendenning, 26.

Content Consultants
Dr. Virgina L. Naples, Northern Illinois University

Maria Kent Rowell, Science Consultant, Sebastopol, California

David Larwa, National Science Education Consultant, Educational Training Services Brighton, Michigan

This book supports the National Science Standards.

Contents

Range Map for Sloths..4

A Quick Look at Sloths...5

What Are Sloths?..7

What Sloths Eat 15

A Sloth's Life 19

The Future of Sloths..25

Photo Diagram 28

Glossary 30

Internet Sites, Address, Books to Read 31

Index...32

MEXICO

BELIZE
HONDURAS
GUATEMALA   NICARAGUA
EL SALVADOR   Caribbean
Sea

North
Atlantic
Ocean

COSTA RICA   VENEZUELA   GUYANA
SURINAME

PANAMA   FRENCH
GUIANA
COLOMBIA   (FRANCE)

ECUADOR

AMAZON
RIVER
PERU   BRAZIL

Range
of the Sloth

BOLIVIA

Surrounding
Land

South
Pacific
Ocean

PARAGUAY

CHILE

Water

South
Atlantic
Ocean

Borders

Rivers

ARGENTINA   URUGUAY

N
W   E
S

A Quick Look at Sloths

What do sloths look like?

Sloths have small heads and long legs. They have hairy bodies that are often green in the rainy season. That is because algae grow in sloth fur. Algae are small, simple plants that have no roots or stems. They grow in wet places.

Where do sloths live?

Sloths live in the trees in the rain forests of Central and South America. Two-toed sloths are called unau (YOO-naw). They live mainly in Central America. Three-toed sloths are called ai. They live mainly in South America.

What do sloths eat?

Sloths eat plants, including twigs, leaves, and berries. They get their water mainly by eating juicy leaves, or by licking water drops from leaves.

Sloths spend most of their lives hanging upside down from trees.

What Are Sloths?

Sloths have lived on Earth for millions of years. They are the slowest moving **mammals** in the world. Mammals have fur, and female mammals feed their young milk. Mammals are also warm-blooded. A warm-blooded animal's body temperature stays the same even when it is hot or cold outside. Unlike most other mammals, a sloth's temperature rises a little if it is warm outside. It also lowers if it is cool outside or if the sloth is still. This change in temperature helps sloths save energy.

Sloths are **arboreal**. This means they live mainly in trees. Sloths rest or sleep in forks in trees. They also spend time hanging upside down.

The fur of this sloth looks greenish because algae is growing on it.

Appearance

All kinds of sloths look alike in some ways. They have small round heads and small ears. They have large eyes and flat faces. Their short bodies are covered with long hair that is gray, brown, or tan. Each kind of sloth has different markings. The maned sloth has an extra long growth of thick hair around its head.

Did you know that as many as 900 species of moths, beetles, and other insects have been found living in a sloth's fur? They eat the algae that grows on a sloth's fur.

Sloth hair is different from the hair of most other mammals. It grows toward the back instead of toward the belly. This growth helps rainwater run off when sloths hang upside down.

Every hair on a sloth is grooved. A groove is a long cut in the surface of something. In the rainy season, algae grow in these grooves. Algae are small, simple plants that have no roots or stems. They grow in wet places. Algae make a sloth's fur look green. This helps sloths blend in with trees so their enemies cannot see them. Colors, shapes, and patterns that help a living thing blend into a background are called **camouflage**.

Sloth bodies are built for living upside down in the trees. Their long arms and claws help them hold onto branches. The skin on their hands and feet is thick and tough. It is not hurt by rough bark.

Kinds of Sloths

Sloths are divided into two groups, the two-toed sloths and the three-toed sloths. Altogether, there are five **species** of sloths. A species is group of animals or plants closely related to each other. Two-toed sloths are more than 2 feet (.6 m) long and weigh up to 18 pounds (8.5 kg). They have no tails. Their arms are a little longer than their legs. Each arm and leg has two toes, joined together with skin. Long, curved claws grow from each toe.

Three-toed sloths are smaller than two-toed sloths. They are usually less than 2 feet (.6 m) long and weigh up to 10 pounds (5 kg). They have short tails. Their arms are longer than their legs. Each arm and leg has three toes joined together with skin. A long claw grows from each toe.

Two-toed and three-toed sloths have different numbers of vertebrae. Vertebrae are the small bones that make up a backbone. Three-toed sloths have more vertebrae. The extra vertebrae give three-toed sloths longer necks. They also let them turn their heads almost all the way around.

You can see the long curved claws on this two-toed sloth.

Two-toed sloths are different from three-toed sloths in another way. Two-toed sloths are active only at night. They often move from tree to tree. Three-toed sloths are active during the day and at night. They do not move as often from tree to tree.

Sloths pull themselves forward when they travel on land.

A Sloth's Speed

The word sloth means laziness. Why are sloths called lazy? They got their name because they sleep a lot. They also move slowly. Sloths do not need to travel far to find food or resting places in the trees. They move slowly to save energy.

Sloths can move faster in the trees than on the ground. If they need to, sloths can move up to 100 feet (30 m) per minute in the trees. On the ground, they can move about 12 feet (3.6 m) per minute.

Where Sloths Live

Sloths live in Central and South America. Two-toed sloths live mainly in Central America. Three-toed sloths live mainly in South America.

Sloths live in warm rain forests. Rain forests are places where many different kinds of trees and plants grow close together and a lot of rain falls.

Sloths live mainly in the rain forest **canopy**. The canopy is a thick area of leaves high up in the treetops. The canopy has lower, middle, and upper parts. The lower and middle canopy is from 20 feet (6 m) to 100 feet (30 m) above the ground. The upper canopy is about 150 feet (46 m) above the ground.

Sloths do not leave the canopy often. Everything they need is there. They have leaves and plants to eat. They drink water that collects on leaves and branches.

This three-toed sloth is getting moisture by eating a leaf.

What Sloths Eat

Sloths are herbivores. Herbivores are animals that eat only plants. Sloths eat leaves and buds. A bud is the part of a plant that grows into a leaf or flower. Sloths also eat twigs and fruits. They have strong jaws for chewing.

Sloths do not eat all the kinds of plants available to them. Three-toed sloths are the most choosy. Two-toed sloths eat more kinds of plants.

Sloth mothers share partially chewed leaves with their young. These kinds of leaves become the young sloths' favorite foods.

Because sloths live in trees, they do not often drink from pools of water on the ground. They get their water from juicy leaves, or by licking water drops from leaves.

This sloth is using its lips and mouth to grab leaves from the tree.

Finding Food

Sloths spend their lives looking for food in their **home ranges**. A home range is an area close to where an animal is born. Animals live and hunt in their home ranges. A three-toed sloth has a home range of about 5 acres (2 ha). The range of a two-toed sloth is about 10 acres (4 ha). Sloths travel about 125 feet (38 m) or less each day.

Sloths use their claws or lips to grab food. They use their thick lips to pull leaves, flowers, and fruit from the trees. They use their side teeth to chew.

Sloths spend much of their time sleeping. This means they do not use a lot of energy. It also means they do not need lots of food. When sloths do eat, their bodies digest the food slowly. To digest means to break down food so the body can use it. It may take a few days for a sloth to digest one meal.

Scientists think three-toed sloths like this one make wailing sounds to find mates.

A Sloth's Life

Sometimes two or more female two-toed sloths live together in one tree. But sloths usually live and travel alone. They come together only to mate.

Sloths cannot mate until they are fully grown. Males are fully grown when they are four to five years old. Females are fully grown when they are three years old. Females give birth to one young per year, usually during the rainy season.

Scientists are not sure how male and female sloths find each other for mating. They think sloths make special noises to find mates. Three-toed sloths, for example, make wailing sounds during mating season. Sloths may also rub their scents on the tree branches.

A This mother sloth is carrying her young through the trees.

Young Sloths

Six to 11 months after mating, females give birth. They give birth hanging upside down in trees. Newborns are about 10 inches (25 cm) long and weigh about 12 ounces (340 g).

Newborns use their claws to hold onto the mother's long hair. The newborn rides on the mother for up to nine months. During this time, the mother feeds her young leaves and milk from her body. This is called nursing, something common to all mammals.

After nine months, the young are strong enough to move around on their own. The mother usually leaves the part of her home range where her young remain. Often, a young sloth will eventually move away to find its own home range.

In the wild, sloths live about 12 to 15 years. Sloths in zoos can live up to 40 years.

Avoiding Predators

A sloth's **predators** include jaguars, ocelots, snakes, and harpy eagles. In the rainy season, a sloth's green fur helps it hide in the canopy.

Resting in the forks of trees also helps sloths hide. They curl into a ball. This makes them look like termite nests or knots on the tree. They are hard to see this way. If predators find them, sloths bite and scratch.

▲ This sloth is swimming across a river to travel to another part of the rain forest.

What Is a Sloth's Day Like?

Sloths spend up to 15 hours each day sleeping. They do not sleep in nests or holes in trees. They curl up in tree forks or hang upside down from tree branches. Two-toed sloths usually move to a new tree each day. Three-toed sloths may stay in one tree for several days.

Sloths pull themselves along tree branches, hand over hand. Sometimes tree branches are too far apart for sloths to reach another tree. Then, they climb down the tree trunk to the ground. Sloths have less muscle than other mammals. They don't need lots of muscles to hang upside down. Only young sloths can stand and then for short periods of time. Sloths cannot walk. They must lie on their bellies and pull themselves along the ground with their claws.

On the ground, sloths can move only 15 yards (14 m) each minute. Sloths face the greatest danger from predators when they are on the ground. Predators are animals that hunt other animals and eat them.

Sometimes sloths swim to new areas of their home ranges. Sloths are excellent swimmers. They swim face down through the water. Water flows off their coats, making it easier to move.

This sloth is sleeping in its habitat. Sloths need rain forest trees to live.

The Future of Sloths

There once were more species of sloths in the world. Some were the size of elephants or larger. These giant ground sloths became **extinct**. Extinct means there are no sloths from those species alive today.

Today, sloths are in danger because people are cutting down the rain forests. People use the land. They build houses, grow crops, and graze cattle. They also sell the wood from the trees. When the rain forest is cut down, many sloths lose their **habitats**. A habitat is a place where an animal or plant usually lives. The maned three-toed sloth is losing its habitat in Brazil. It is **endangered**. Endangered means this species may become extinct.

Sloths are safest when they stay in trees. But their homes in rain forest trees are disappearing.

Sloths in the Future

Sloths are in danger from people. Many are run over by cars or trucks when they try to cross roads.

Scientists are not sure how many sloths live in the wild today. They think the number of wild sloths around the world is falling.

Some people are trying to save sloths. They bring sloths to live in zoos or in preserves. A preserve is a place where it is against the law to hunt animals.

Some scientists catch sloths to learn more about them. They try to learn new ways to help sloths live in places other than their natural habitats.

Many people understand that sloths are important to life in the rain forests. Sometimes these people teach other people what they know. Together, people can use what they learn to help keep sloths alive in their rain forest homes.

long limbs
see page 10

fur-covered body
see page 9

hands and feet
see page 9

head and face
see page 8

Glossary

algae (AL-jee)—small plants or plant-like life without roots, stems, or leaves that grows in wet places

arboreal (ar-BOH-ree-uhl)—living mainly in trees

camouflage (KAM-uh-flahj)—coloring or a covering that makes something look like its surroundings

canopy (KAN-uh-pee)—a thick area of leaves high up in the treetops, like a giant umbrella

endangered (en-DAYN-jurd)—in danger of dying out

extinct (ek-STINGKT)—a species that has died out

habitat (HAB-i-tat)—the native environment of an animal or plant

home range (HOME RAYNJ)—an area where an animal has found all the things it needs to live

mammal (MAM-uhl)—a warm-blooded animal with a backbone that breathes air

predator (PRED-uh-tur)—an animal that hunts and eats other animals

species (SPEE-seez)—one of the groups into which animals and plants are divided according to their likenesses

Internet Sites

The Sloth Web Site
http://www.geocities.com/Hollywood/Set/1478/
 sloth.html

Sloths.org
http://www.sazoo-aq.org/sloth.html

Useful Address

Rainforest Action Network
2221 Pine Street
Suite 500
San Francisco, CA 94104

Books to Read

Bach, Julie. *Sloths.* Mankato, MN: Creative
 Education, 1999.

Paige, Joy. *The Sloth: The World's Slowest
 Mammal.* New York: Powerkids Press, 2001.

Index

algae, 5, 9
arboreal, 7

bark, 9

camouflage, 9
canopy, 13, 21
Central America, 13
claw, 9, 10, 17, 20, 23

endangered, 25
extinct, 25

giant ground sloth, 25

habitat, 25, 27
home range, 17, 21, 23
herbivore, 15

mammal, 7, 9, 21, 23

nursing, 21

predator, 21, 23
preserve, 27

rainwater, 9

scientist, 19, 27
South America, 13
species, 10, 25

temperature, 7

unau, 5

vertebrae, 10

warm-blooded, 7

zoo, 21, 27